A MARTIN SCORSESE FILM

HUGO

MUSIC FROM THE ORIGINAL SCORE

MUSIC BY HOWARD SHORE

ISBN 978-1-4584-2054-1

HAL•LEONARD®
CORPORATION

7777 W. BLUEMOUND RD. P.O. BOX 13819 MILWAUKEE, WI 53213

In Australia Contact:
Hal Leonard Australia Pty. Ltd.
4 Lentara Court
Cheltenham, Victoria, 3192 Australia
Email: ausadmin@halleonard.com.au

Visit Hal Leonard Online at
www.halleonard.com

CONTENTS

THE THIEF

By HOWARD SHORE

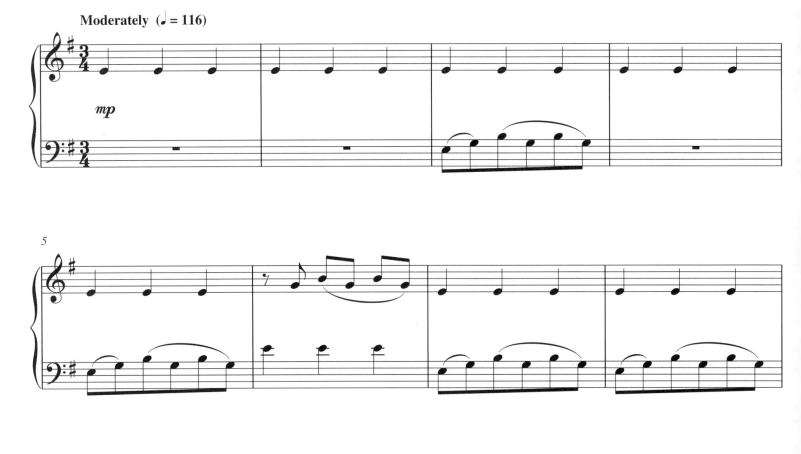

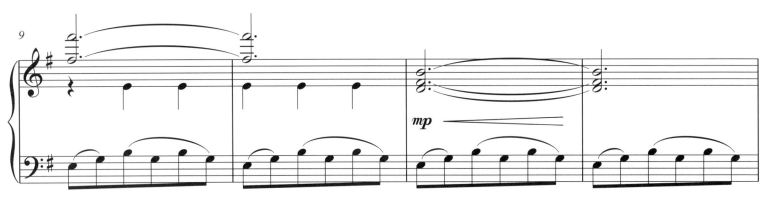

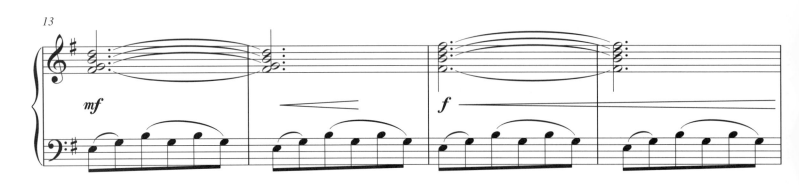

THE CHASE

By HOWARD SHORE
Contains an excerpt from "Ça Gaze"
by V. MARCEAU

Easily, in 2 (♩. = 124)

THE CLOCKS

By HOWARD SHORE
Contains an excerpt from "Aubade Charmeuse"
by JEAN PEYRONNIN

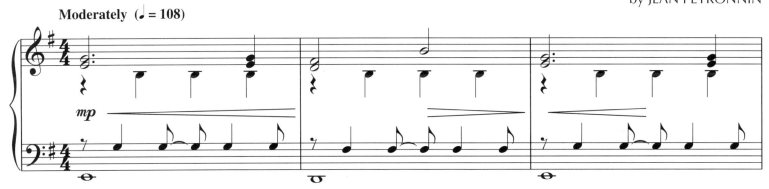

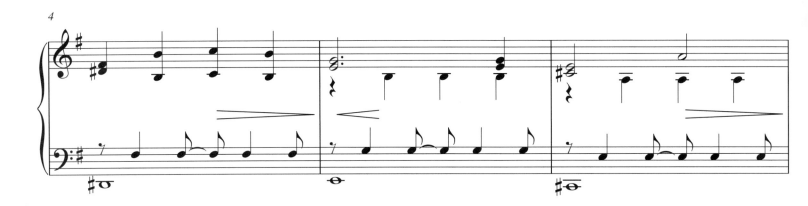

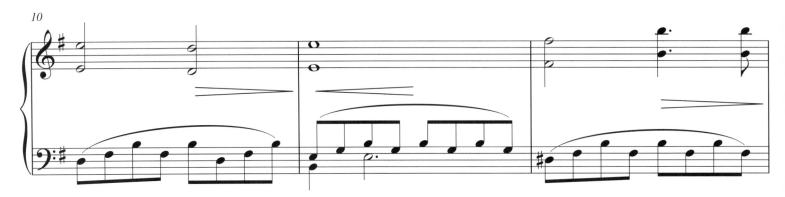

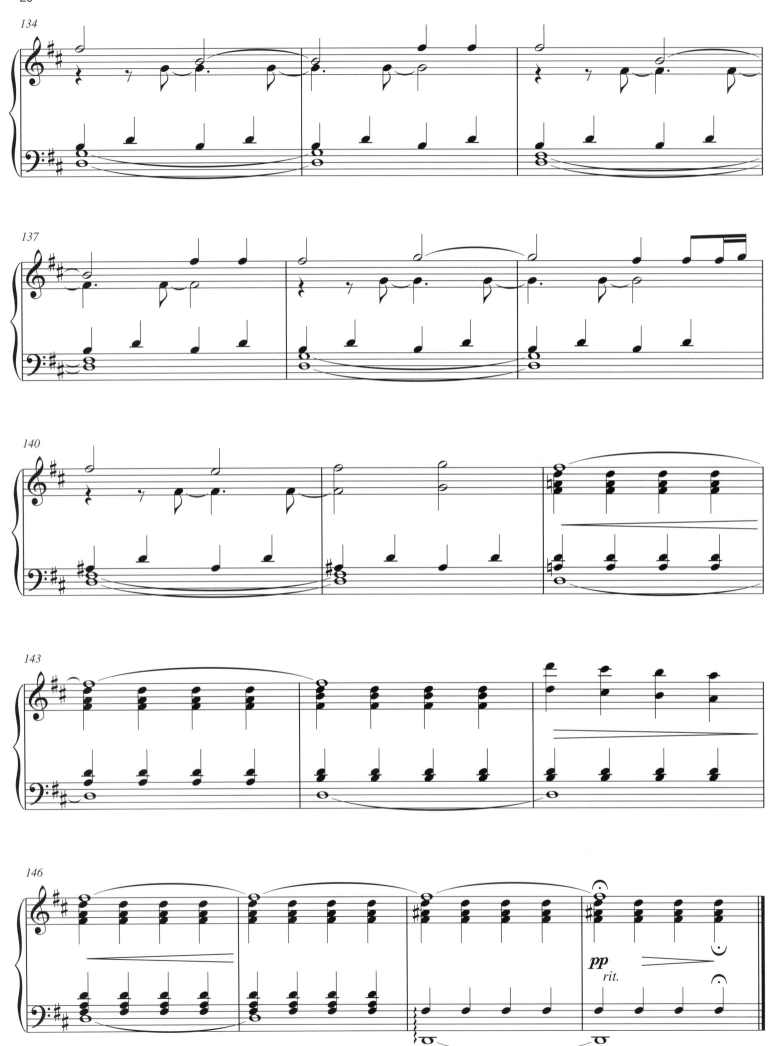

SNOWFALL

By HOWARD SHORE

Moderately (♩ = 120)

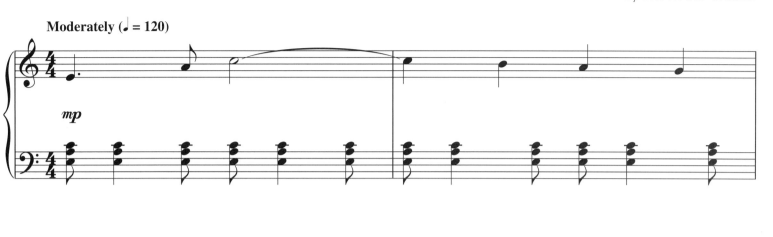

HUGO'S FATHER

By HOWARD SHORE

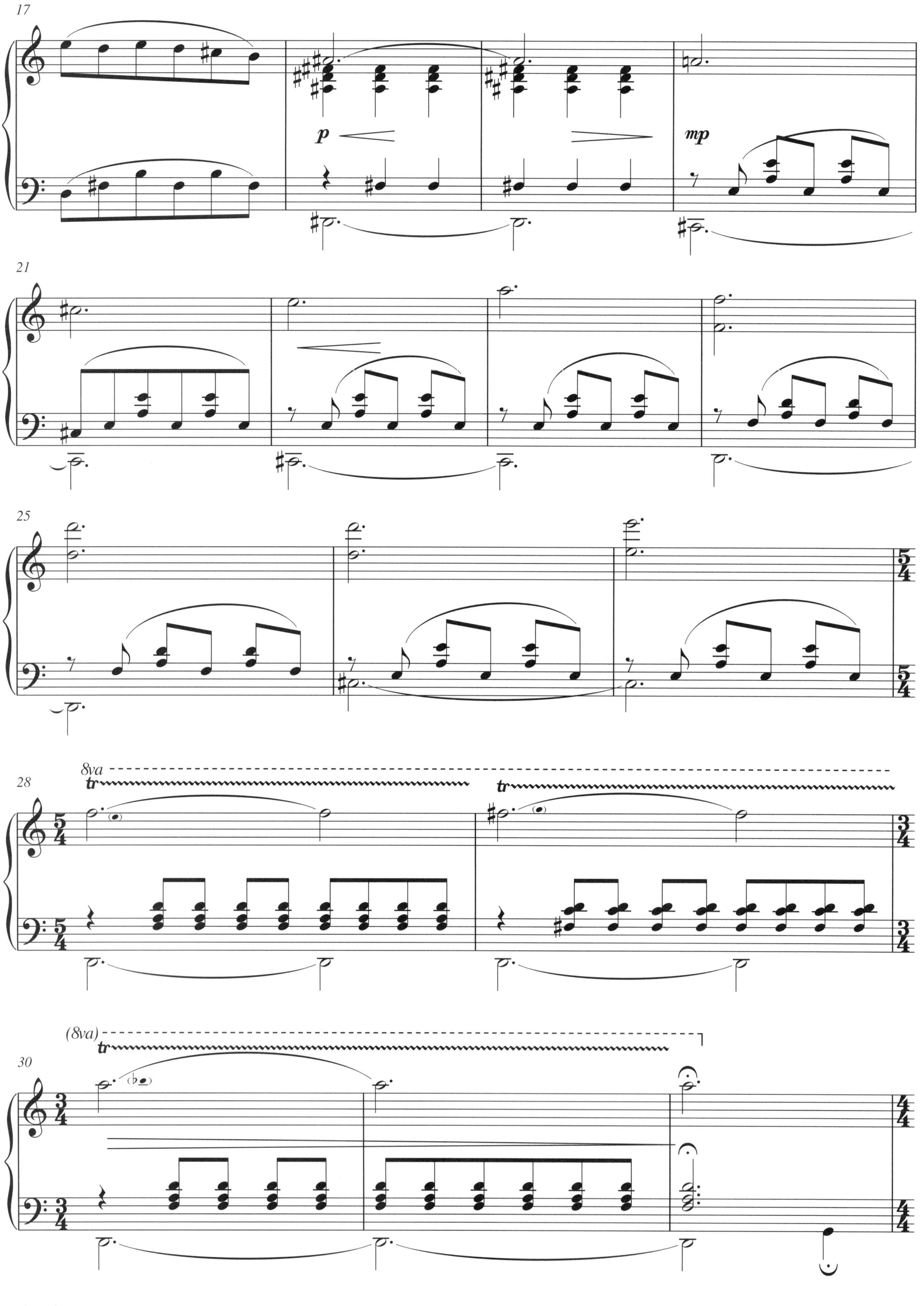
17
p
mp
21
25
28
8va
tr
tr
30
(8va)
tr

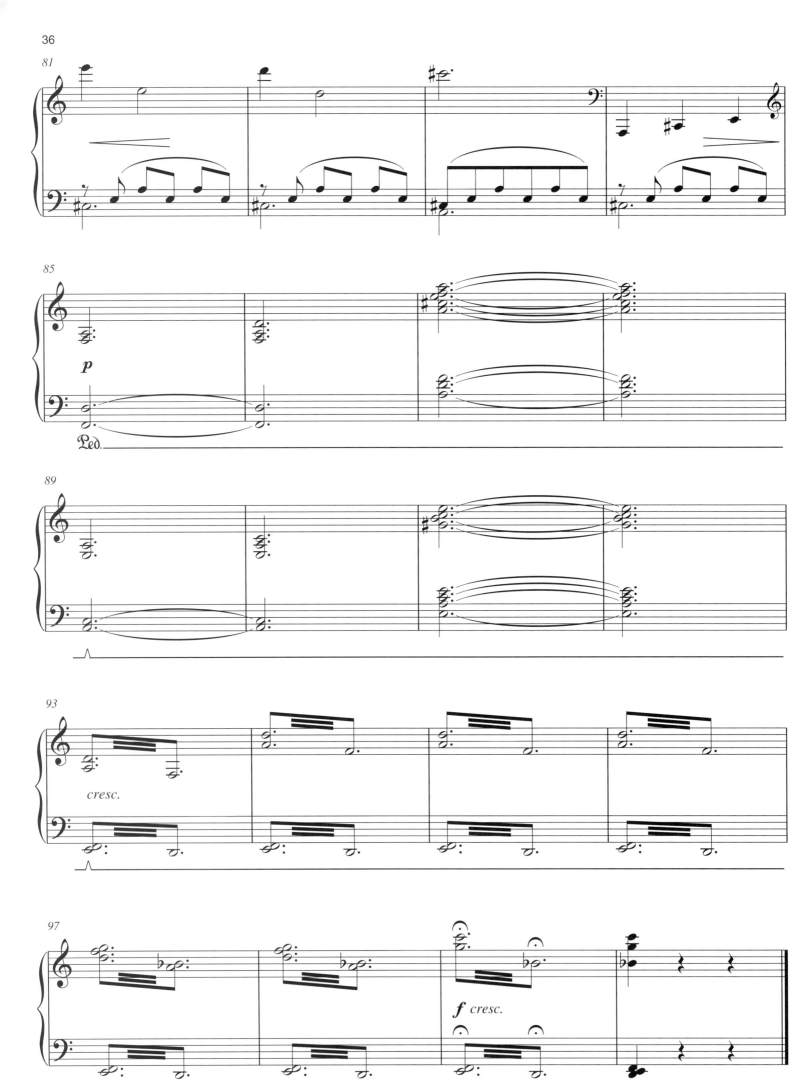

ASHES

By HOWARD SHORE

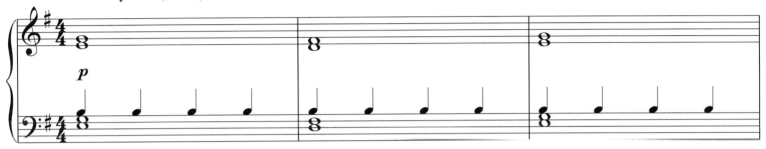

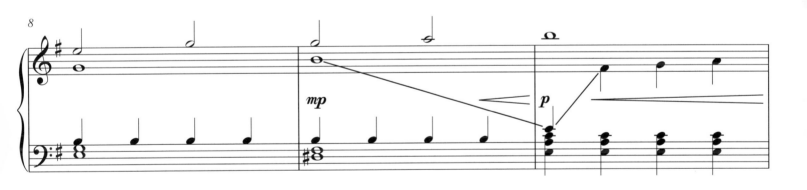

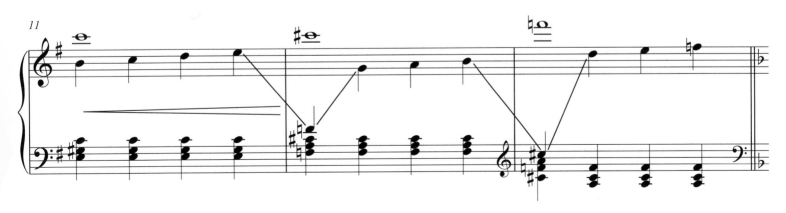

THE STATION INSPECTOR

By HOWARD SHORE

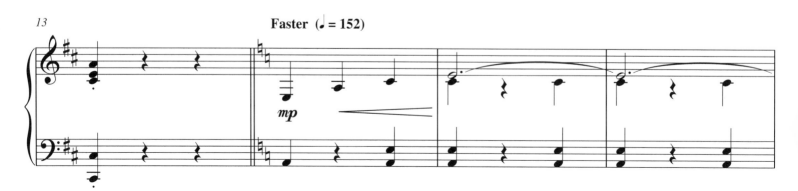

THE PLAN

By HOWARD SHORE

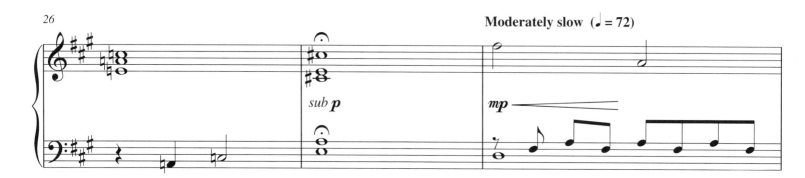

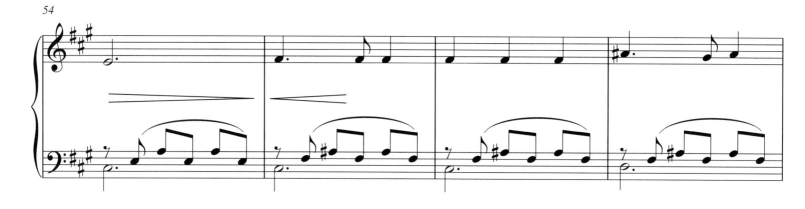

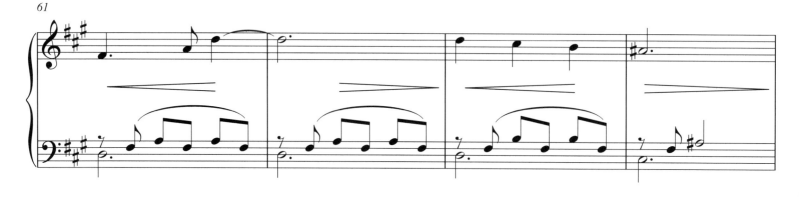

PAPA GEORGES MADE MOVIES

By HOWARD SHORE

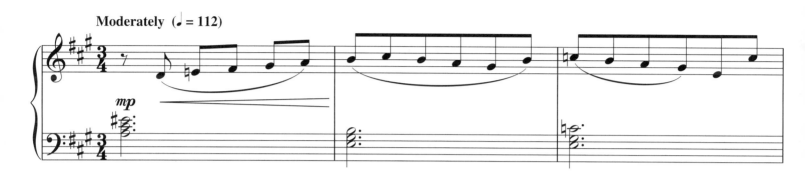

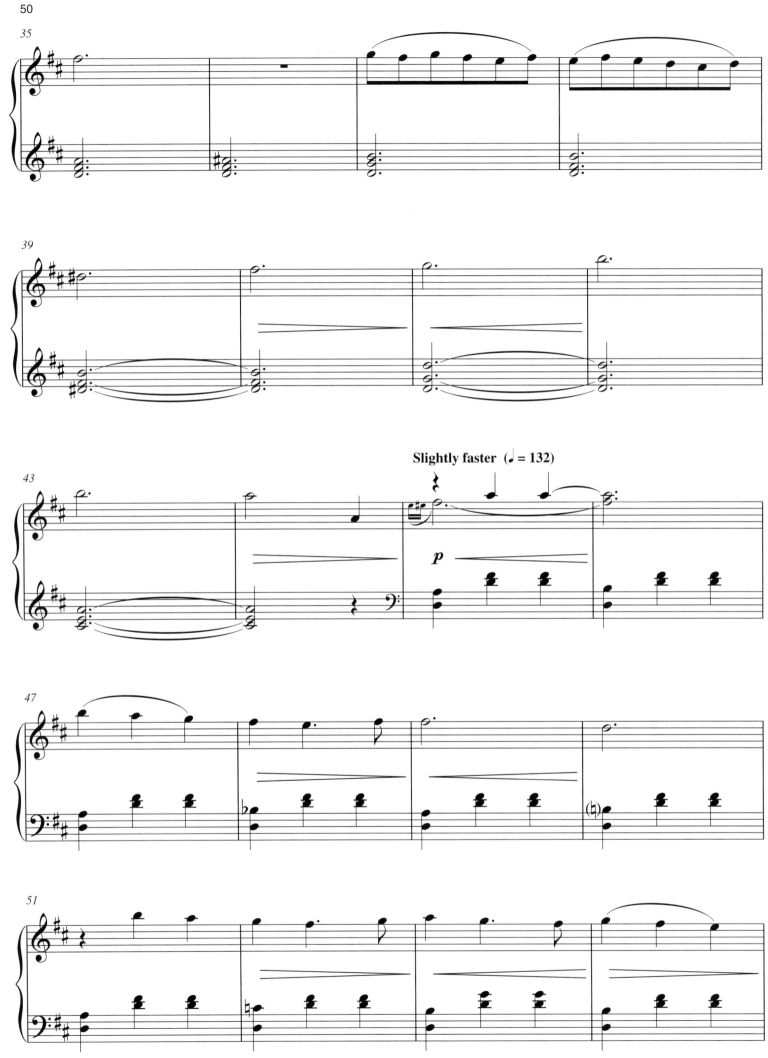

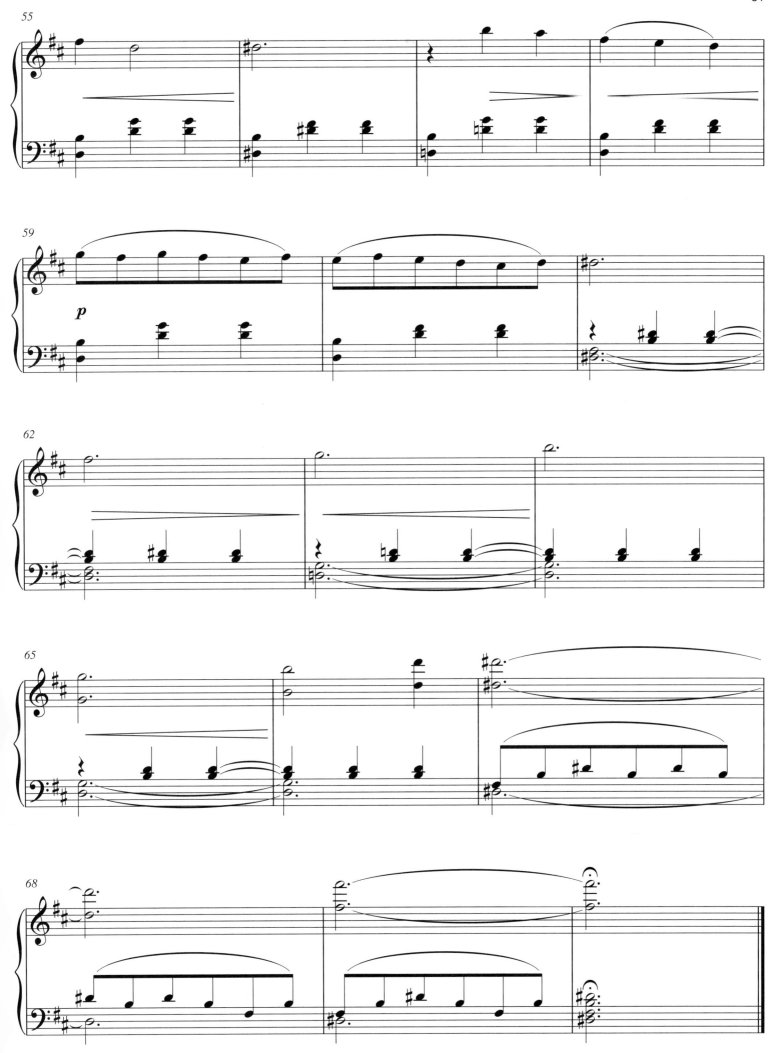

A GHOST IN THE STATION

By HOWARD SHORE

Moderately fast (♩ = 168)

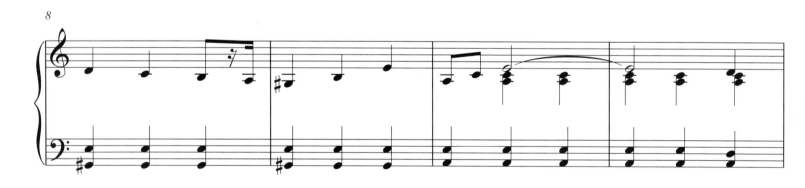

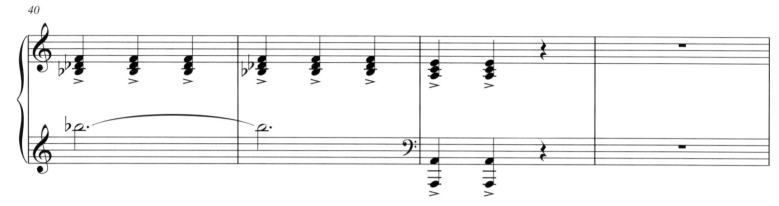

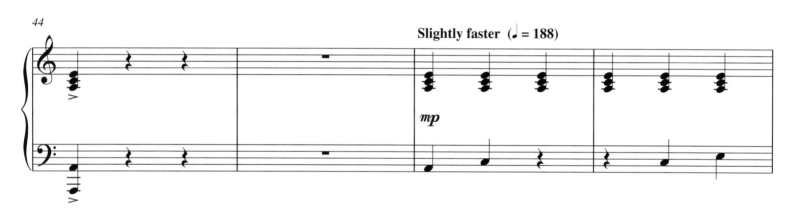

THE MAGICIAN

By HOWARD SHORE

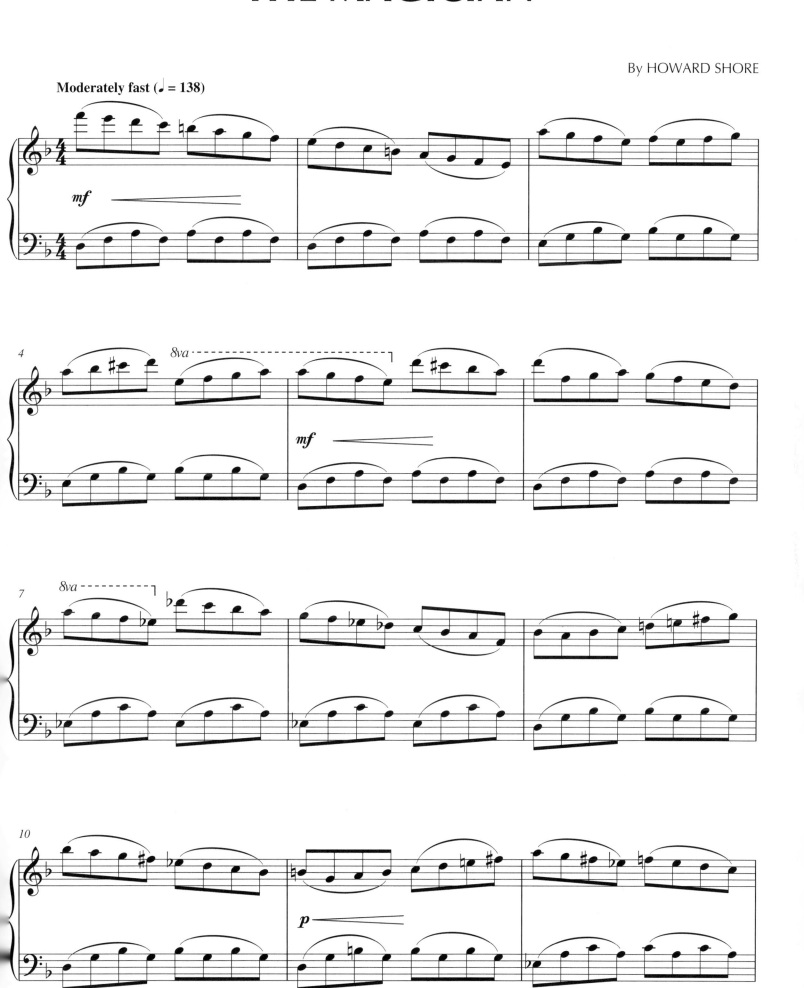

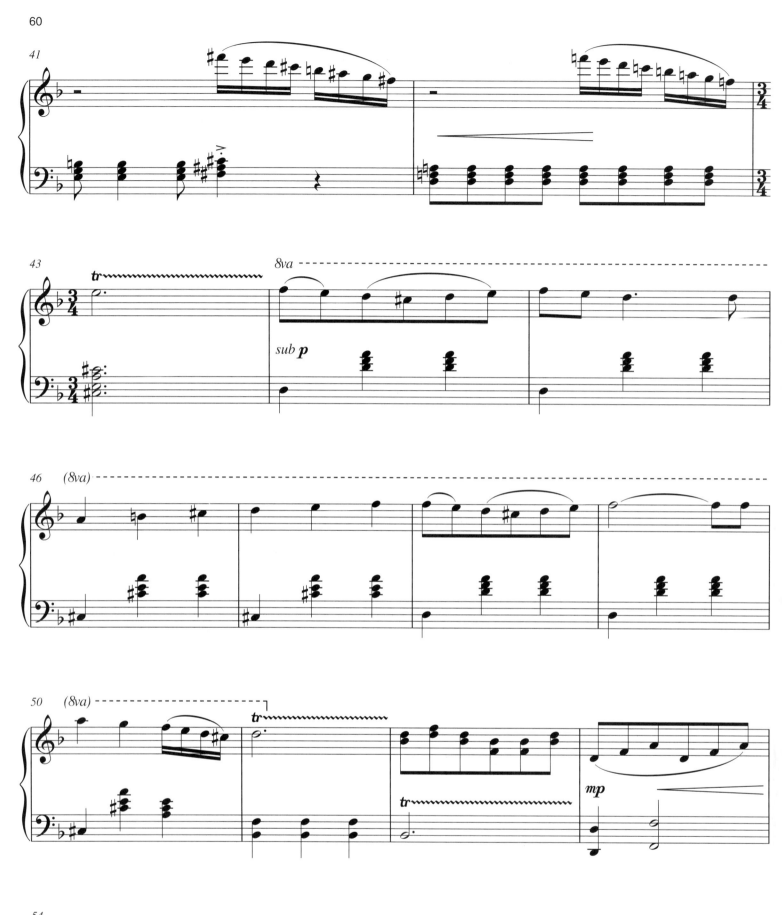

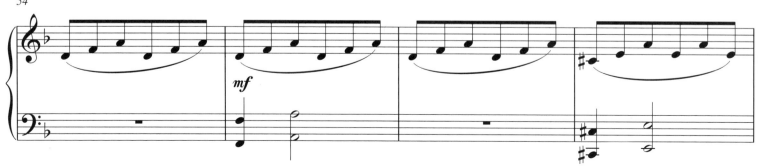

COEUR VOLANT

By ELIZABETH COTNOIR,
ISABELLE GEFFROY, HOWARD SHORE

64